kandahar

PROVINCIAL HANDBOOK / A Guide to the People and the Province

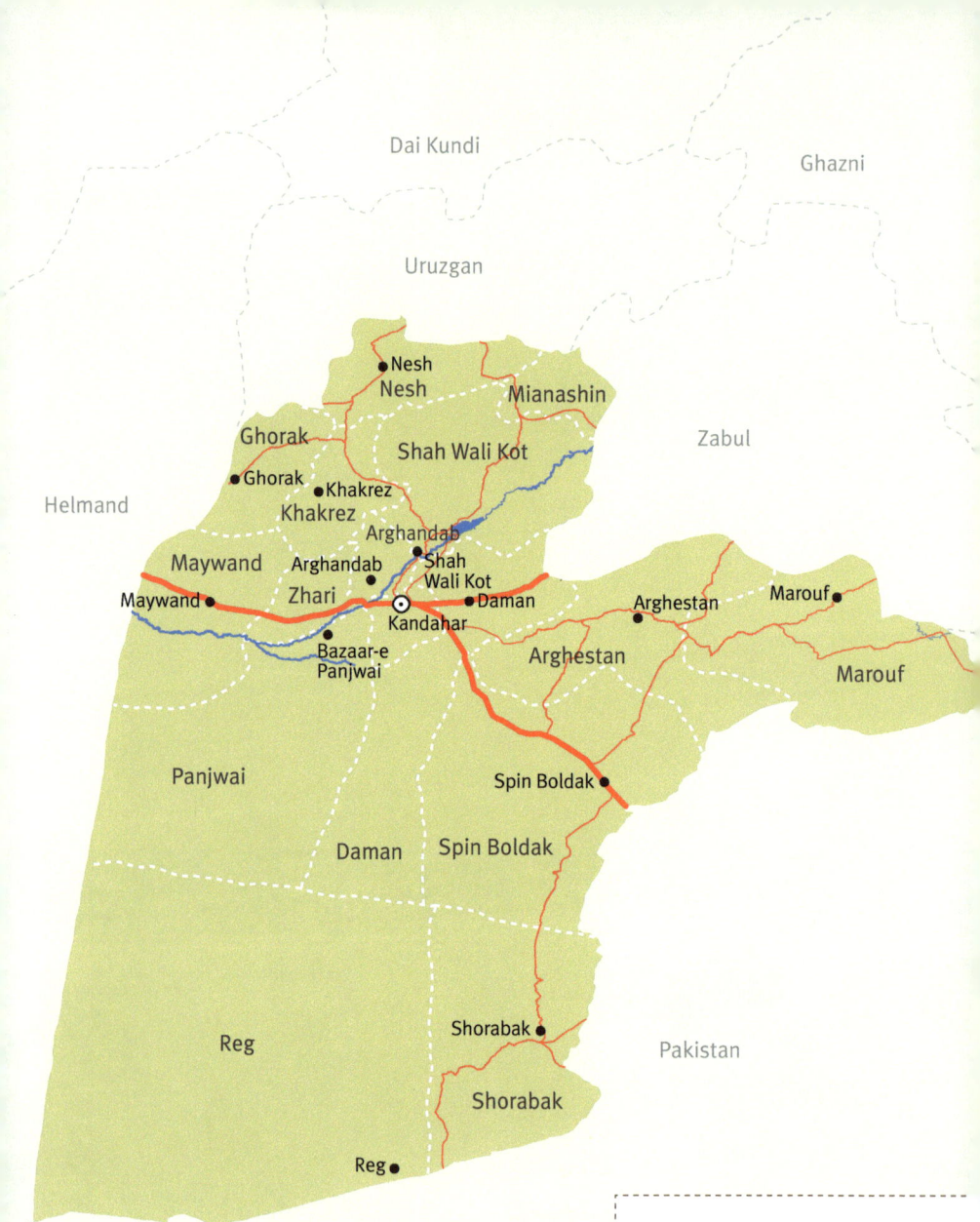

Dai Kundi

Ghazni

Uruzgan

Zabul

Helmand

- Nesh
Nesh

Mianashin

Shah Wali Kot

Ghorak
- Ghorak

- Khakrez
Khakrez

Arghandab
- Arghandab
- Shah Wali Kot

Maywand
- Maywand

Zhari

⊙ Kandahar

- Daman

Arghestan
- Arghestan

Marouf
- Marouf

Marouf

- Bazaar-e Panjwai

Panjwai

Daman

Spin Boldak
- Spin Boldak

Spin Boldak

Reg

Shorabak
- Shorabak

Pakistan

Shorabak

Reg
- Reg

Kandahar

▬▬	Roads
▭▭	District Border
▬▬	River
⊙	Provincial Center
•	City
	District Name

Table of Contents

List of Tables and Maps

Guide to the Handbook

This handbook is intended to be a concise field guide to Kandahar for internationals deploying to the province. Reading the guide will accelerate the orientation process and help readers better think about the challenges of Kandahar province throughout their time in the field.

Key sources for this guide include official Islamic Republic of Afghanistan (IRoA), United Nations, and United States government (USG) publications. The book also reflects information and perspectives from Afghan and international experts who have spent significant time in Kandahar.

The editors made every effort to ensure accuracy within the deadlines. It should be noted, however, that there is often considerable disagreement regarding what is "ground truth" in Afghanistan, and things are constantly changing. As such, consider this book part of your orientation, not the all-inclusive answer to what you need to know. The best information is from those individuals and organizations in Kandahar who know it inside and out. The handbook suggests resources and organizations that can further assist. There also is a list of recommended references and internet sites listed in the Appendix.

Information in this handbook is unclassified. The views and opinions expressed in this handbook are those of IDS International and in no way reflect the views of the United States Government or the United States Army.

HOW TO USE THE HANDBOOK

To help stabilize a community, it is necessary to understand that community – its people, history, culture, economy, interests, and needs. Military operations alone are insufficient in counterinsurgency. Understanding the community will assist the creation of a civil affairs strategy – in partnership with the Provincial Reconstruction Team (PRT) and the Afghans themselves – to address sources of instability in the province. Understanding the community and working effectively with local groups and governments can help separate the insurgency from the population and lay the groundwork for lasting stability. It is essential not only to know who matters within a community, but also what type of assistance or engagement would be most effective, and what political compromises are possible.

Here are some questions that apply to engaging communities in this province:

- What are the influential groups in my area (tribal, political, business, etc.)?

- What are their interests and relationships? What do they care most about and why? What are their perceptions of themselves, their neighbors, the IRoA, and international forces/activities in their area?

- How can that community or group be more connected to the larger political process of creating a representative and responsive Afghan government? What political or economic issues must be addressed to create effective governance responsive to this community?

- What are the sources of conflict or instability in this area? Are groups pursuing interests in a way that fosters conflict or undermines stability or governance? If so, why?

- Are you communicating with the right representatives of that group? How can you establish and maintain credibility with the group? How can you use our influence, operations, leverage and resources to address sources of conflict and instability and to connect that community to the process of building a stable Afghanistan?

THE ELECTRONIC UPDATE

Look for electronic updates to this book at *www.idsinternational.net/ afpakbooks*. Updates will cover any new developments, issues, and leaders that have emerged after publication. They will also provide corrections and expanded content in key areas based on feedback from readers.

We hope the handbook will continue to be a valuable tool in thinking about the challenges in Kandahar. If you have questions, comments, or feedback for the update or future editions, please email afghanbooks@idsinternational.net.

ABOUT IDS INTERNATIONAL – PUBLISHER OF AFGHANISTAN EASTERN REGION SERIES

This book is one of two handbooks on the provinces of Afghanistan's Southern Region: Helmand and Kandahar. In addition to publishing these handbooks, IDS International provides training and analysis to government and private organizations in the areas of politics, economics, culture, stability operations, reconstruction, counterinsurgency, and interagency relations. In particular, IDS is a leading trainer of the US military on working with Provincial Reconstruction Teams (PRTs) in Iraq and Afghanistan. IDS offers its clients expertise and experience in the difficult work of interagency collaboration in complex operations. The writers and editors on this project bring a lifetime of experience working in these provinces and share a dedication to bring peace and prosperity to the people of Afghanistan.

Editors: Nick Dowling, Tom Praster and Dana Stinson
Assistant Editor: Tom Viehe; **Research:** Josh Adlakha

IDS INTERNATIONAL

1916 Wilson Boulevard

Suite 302

Arlington, VA 22201

703-875-2212

www.idsinternational.net

afghanbooks@idsinternational.net

PUBLISHED: DECEMBER 2008

Although the province is historically famous for fruits such as pomegranates and apricots, years of drought and war have destroyed many of Kandahar's orchards and eroded a substantial backbone to the province's livelihood.

PHOTO BY LUCAS ROBINSON

Chapter 1
Overview, Orientation and History

From the air, Kandahar appears to be empty, with just the stark beauty of open sand or rolling hills and few human dwellings. But the aerial view is deceptive because hidden in every crevice is a river valley bursting with green fields and crowded with people. The routes and river valleys of Kandahar have recently become arguably the toughest battle-fields in Afghanistan, but this province has held a prominent place in history for centuries. The Pashtuns who dominate this region trace their lineage back to the time of Alexander the Great. Kandaharis frequently tell visitors of their province's role in the political upheavals that have swept through Afghanistan over the years, and it seems natural to them that Kandahar stands at the heart of the latest conflagration.

Afghanistan's founding father, Ahmed Shah Durrani (affectionately called "Ahmed Shah Baba," or Father Ahmed Shah) made Kandahar his capital. Durrani brought to the city an ancient cloak that was believed to have belonged to the Prophet Mohammed, a holy relic that remains sealed in an ornate shrine. Kandaharis took a certain pride in the fact that when the Taliban conquered most of Afghanistan in the early 1990s, they returned Kandahar to its historical role as Afghanistan's capital city. President Hamid Karzai has invoked this same sense of history with billboards around Kandahar, showing a picture of Durrani next to his own portrait.

Rural people in Kandahar follow their ancient traditions far more closely than they might in other parts of Afghanistan. They harvest grapes and pomegranates, keep their women hidden behind mud walls, and observe the Islamic prayers and fasts with devotion. However, a few trappings of the modern world have spread to the countryside, including mobile phones and diesel-fueled irrigation pumps.

Life is different in Kandahar City. Young men wearing jeans and T-shirts lounge around pool tables, pornography is sold on the black market, and fitness clubs cater to the growing popularity of bodybuilding. Paintings of American movie heroes decorate the backs of the three-wheeled taxi motorbikes. These signs of modernity are only a colorful layer on the surface of Kandahar's culture, however. Underneath lies an historical province that follows ancient rules.

ORIENTATION

Located in southern Afghanistan, Kandahar is bordered by three Afghan provinces – Helmand, Uruzgan, and Zabul – and the Pakistani province of Baluchistan. Most of the province's 47,000 square kilometers is dominated by flatlands, with about eight percent of its surface area to the north covered by mountains rising more than 2,500 meters above sea level. More rocky spines emerge from the dust further south, and the sharp hills of De Kowtal Murcheh Ghar, Kan-e Tella Ghar, Zareh Shar Ghar, and Zaker Ghar Shomali serve as natural protection for Kandahar City.

Important routes pass through, or near, Kandahar City. The paved, two-lane Ring Road (Highway 1) heading west is known as the Herat Road, and the portion heading east is "the Kabul Road." The other major paved road leading north to Tirin Kot, the capital of Uruzgan province, is "Tirin Kot or TK Road;" and southeast through the district of Spin Boldak to the Pakistani border town of Chaman is Highway 4, frequently called the "Boldak" or "Chaman" Road.

River valleys also serve as transit routes, partly because during the majority of the year their sandy beds are smooth corridors for travel. The biggest river, the Arghandab, flows from Lake Arghandab ("Band-e Arghandab") in the Shah Wali Kot district, travels south through the Arghandab district, curves southwest as it passes near Kandahar City, and continues west where it joins the other major river, the Dowrey Rud, before finally leaving the province through the western district of Maywand. Arghandab's river corridor has been a nexus for the insurgency in recent years and also serves as a major drug trafficking route.

About one million people live in Kandahar province. The population is almost entirely Pashtun, with perhaps two percent of Baluch, Tajik, Hazara, and others. The Afghan government officially recognizes 2,847 villages in the province, but formal village names often refer to areas that locals consider clusters of villages, each with different names and identities. Three decades of urbanization, such as the growth of ramshackle slums on the south and north sides of Kandahar City, have shifted Kandahar's population from its once rural character. Some estimates suggest that Kandahar City now holds almost half of Kandahar's population.

Districts

There are 16 districts in Kandahar, including the capital district of Kandahar City, although some maps show 17 or 18 districts because the boundaries have changed frequently in recent years. The majority of districts are under the control of Taliban insurgents, with government control reduced to cities and district centers – and in some centers the insurgents have effectively reduced the government's territory to the administration building itself. The government maintains its hold on a few

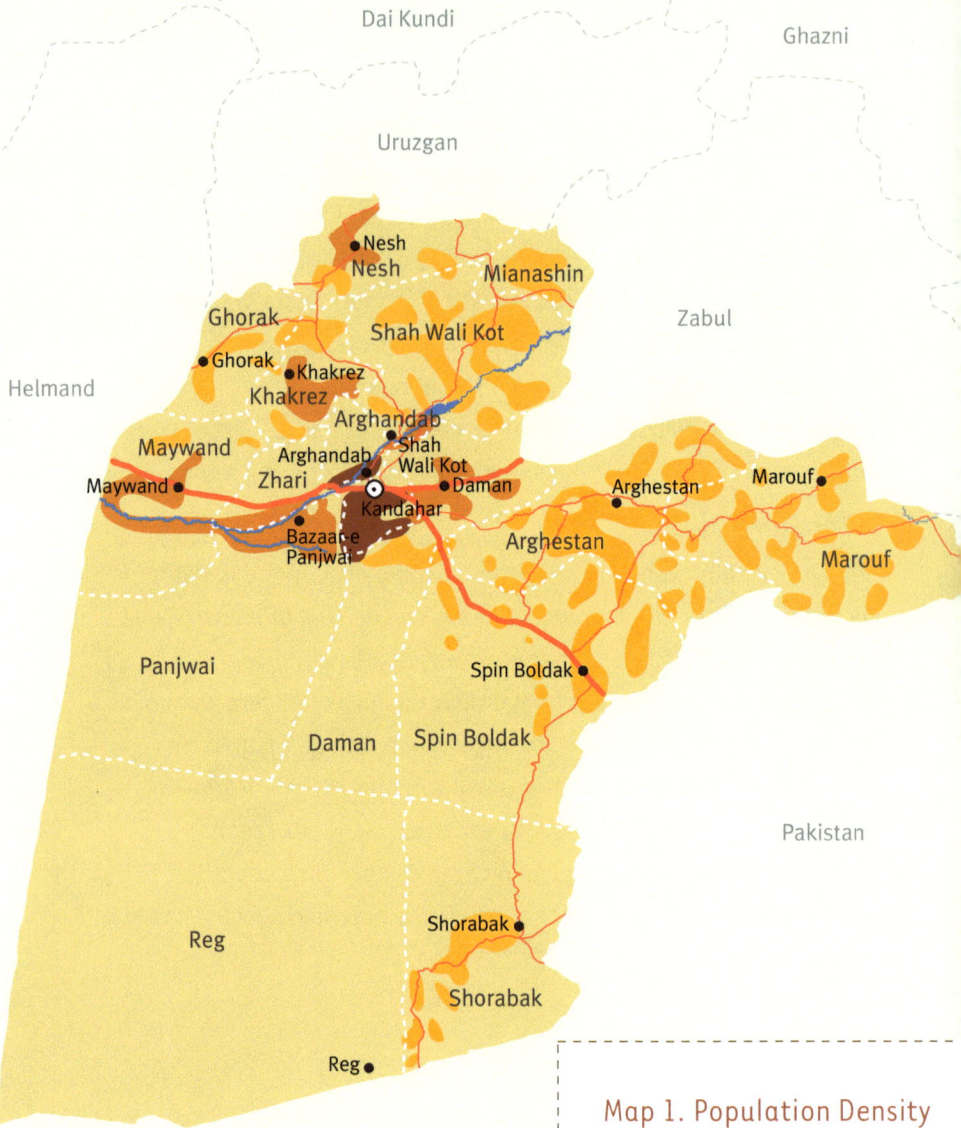

Map 1. Population Density Map of Kandahar

Roads	
District Border	
River	
⊙ Provincial Center	
● City	

LESS — MORE

Table 1. District Populations*

DISTRICT	CENTER	POP. (EST.)	MAJOR TRIBES
Kandahar	Kandahar	490,000	Popolzai, mixed
Spin Boldak	Spin Boldak	103,000	Asakzai, Noorzai
Panjwai	Bazaar-e Panjwai	79,000	Noorzai, Alokazai, Isakzai
Zhari	Zhari	78,000	Panj-pai, mixed
Arghandab	Arghandab	56,000	Alokazai, Ghlizai
Maywand	Maywand	53,000	Noorzai, Isakzai
Shah Wali Kot	Shah Wali Kot	40,000	Popolzai, Alokazai, Barakzai
Daman	Daman	32,000	Popolzai, Barakzai and Ghilzai
Arghestan	Arghestan	31,000	Zirak Durrani group, mixed
Marouf	Marouf	30,000	Barakzai, Alizai and Kakar
Khakrez	Khakrez	21,000	Alokazai, Popolzai
Mianashin	(none)	13,000	Mixed, Hazara
Nesh	Nesh	12,000	Popolzai, Barakzai
Shorabak	Shorabak	10,000	Barech, Baluch
Ghorak	Ghorak	9,000	Alokazai, Popolzai, Barakzai, Isakzai
Reg	(none)	8,000	Baluch

Sources: Population – CSO, Tribes – TLO, LOOK, CAPS, NPS
* This list excludes Dand and Takhta Pul because they are not officially recognized as districts.

districts in the center of the province, but those zones are under serious pressure from the insurgency. A few districts, such as Arghestan and Reg, are considered by some analysts to be "locally-controlled," meaning they are under the influence of independent tribal elders or warlords. Other observers say they should be categorized as Taliban-controlled because many local strongmen have started cooperating with the insurgency.

Kandahar's landcover is mostly rolling desert in the Reg and Shorabak districts, as well as the southern parts of Panjwai, Daman, and Spin Boldak. Further north, the sand stops abruptly and gives way to vast tracts of dusty flatlands in most of Maywand, Zhari, Daman, and Spin Boldak. Climbing into the foothills, the landscape becomes hilly range-land in Arghestan and Marouf, as well as in parts of Ghorak, Khakrez, and Shah Wali Kot. Jagged mountains fringe the northern edge of the province, particularly in Nish and Myanishin. The most politically and strategically important parts of Kandahar are a tiny minority of its surface area, and include the green river valleys that cut through the brown landscape. Especially important is the Arghandab River as it wanders south from Shah Wali Kot into the Arghandab district, and then forms the boundary between Zhari and Panjwai until it leaves Kandahar through the Maywand district.

Key Towns

Kandahar City: Kandahar City, founded by Alexander the Great in the 4th century BC, is a sprawling provincial capital inhabited by half a million people. Kandahar City straddles the major highways that cross southern Afghanistan. The main boulevards are paved, and some of them are lined with trees. Houses in the central neighborhoods have plumbing and electricity. Living conditions worsen sharply in the slums beyond the city's center, where the roads are rutted dirt tracks going through a maze of shanties and children play in the same dirty canals used for waste disposal. Few buildings reach more than two stories, except for the soaring domes of mosques, including the Eid Gah mosque on the north side of the city, and new glass-fronted commercial buildings in the downtown area. The central market, Charsoo, stands at the center of the crumbling old city that was once surrounded by protective walls. To the west, newer neighborhoods (in Shar-i Naw, or the "New City") have grown along two major roads west of Shahidan Chowk, or Martyr's Square, a traffic roundabout that features a small shrine and ornamental cannons.

Spin Boldak: This dusty border town on Highway 4 serves as a waypoint for traders doing business with Pakistan. Rows of metal shutters protect small storage facilities, and highly decorated transport trucks (known as "jingle trucks") crowd the gas pumps. The adjacent smaller town of Wesh, closer to the border itself, is the site of a recently constructed passport office and a newly-established Afghan security post.

Bazaar-e Panjwai: Also known as Panjwai District Center, this town was largely abandoned during major fighting between Taliban and international forces in 2006. It has recently returned to life with the establishment of a major Canadian military outpost, Masum Ghar, on a hill by the same name on the western side of the town. Bazaar-e Panjwai serves as an administrative center and trading hub for the lush Panjwai valley.

Arghandab District Center: This outpost on the south side of the Arghandab River gives the government an important foothold near the rocky outcrops that serve as a natural gateway to the north side of Kandahar city.

RELEVANT HISTORICAL ISSUES

Even an illiterate Kandahari farmer, who likely could not locate the United States on a map, can recite a detailed history of Kandahar. Every history will be told differently, however, because blood feuds that lasted hundreds of years still color the stories that fathers tell their sons.

Ahmed Shah Durrani

The state of Afghanistan was founded in the 18th century during the collapse of two empires: the Safavi dynasty of Iran and the Moghul Empire of India. The city of Kandahar stood at the border of these great civilizations. In 1747, Ahmed Shah Durrani of the Popolzai tribe led a raiding party that ransacked a caravan near Kandahar. He used the plunder to buy support from other tribes and led the Afghans on nine campaigns of conquest, and soon the Popolzai leader controlled much of what is now Iran and Pakistan.

The Durand Line

Memories of the Durrani Empire leave many Afghans feeling entitled to lands beyond their borders. In fact, most Afghans will not use the word "border" when referring to the mountainous divide between their country and Pakistan. The Durand Line was laid down by the British in 1893, and the agreement was to last only 100 years, according to Afghan lore. However, no written versions of the treaty include an expiration date and no international authorities recognize Afghanistan's claims. Kandaharis were rankled in 2002 by Pakistan's construction of the Friendship Gate, an archway that towers over the Wesh-Chaman border crossing, because they saw it as an attempt by Pakistan to seize Afghan land.

The Shah Monarchy (1933-1978)

The relatively peaceful decades under monarchy rule and even the uneasy transition to representative government under Daoud Shah are fondly remembered by the people of Kandahar. Residents describe a time when all major tribes had a role in the government. Naeem Khan, the political and military leader of Kandahar province during those years, was remembered for overseeing the construction of a large textile factory on the eastern outskirts of the city. This factory employed thousands of local people and created a subsidized demand for raw cotton from the fields now dominated by illegal poppy. This period serves as a hopeful reminder that war has not always been a constant fact of life.

Soviet Occupation and the Najibullah Government (1979-1992)

Political turmoil in the 1970s broke into open warfare with the Soviet invasion. Some of the rebel commanders who emerged during this period would continue to influence Kandahar's politics for decades. Mullah Naqib in the Arghandab district became the leader of the powerful Alokazai tribe and continued to play an important role in every subsequent struggle for power in Kandahar. Habibullah Jan, an Alizai tribal commander, carved out a zone of influence west of Kandahar City and later became a member of parliament under the Karzai government. Ustad Abdul Halim rallied anti-Soviet fighters under his leadership in the Marouf district and recently served as a security advisor to the provincial governor. Noorolhaq Olomi, now a member of parliament in Kabul, was a senior communist officer for the southern provinces from 1987 until 1991.

The Afghan government estimates that 50,000 people were killed in the fighting between Soviet and mujahedin forces in Kandahar province. Soviet troops withdrew from Kandahar in 1988. Rebel commanders struck a deal with the government forces that prevented Kandahar City from changing hands until the Najibullah regime finally collapsed. Today, the Taliban draw on military lessons learned during the Soviet occupation as they try to isolate NATO forces in the provincial capital in the same way the communists were eventually besieged. The new Taliban even call themselves "mujahedin," adopting the name of their former enemies to identify their uprising with the anti-Soviet resistance.

Civil War Among Mujahedin (1992-1994)

With the fall of the communist government, rival mujahedin commanders carved up the province, and residents of Kandahar say it was impossible to travel a few city blocks without crossing the battle lines of a bitter civil war. Gul Aga Sherzai assumed the title of provincial governor, but in fact, nobody governed Kandahar. Factories were shut down and trade was stifled by countless checkpoints requiring bribes to cross. Criminality was rampant, and personal feuds spiraled into bloody vendettas. Former mujahedin commanders indulged in sexual excesses, raping women and young boys. Locals stopped referring to them as mujahedin, and started calling them *topakan* or "gun lords." As a measure of dissatisfaction, locals now use this term to refer to the Afghan police.

The Taliban use this history as a powerful propaganda tool against the current Karzai administration, which some locals view as almost as chaotic and predatory. By portraying themselves as bringing security and justice to the countryside, the Taliban insurgents are repeating a successful formula.

Taliban Government (1994-2001)

The Taliban's origins are in Kandahar. In 1994, Mullah Mohammed Omar, a poorly-educated ex-mujahedin fighter who had become a village preacher in Sangisar in Zhari district (west of Kandahar), gathered a group of religious students and mujahedin for a rebellion against the topakan. The outside world was first introduced to the Taliban when they started attacking checkpoints on Highway 1 and guaranteeing safe travel on the road. The Taliban described their goals modestly, saying they wanted only to establish peace and basic justice. They took Kandahar with the consent of Mullah Naqib and other tribal leaders, including the young Hamid Karzai. The Taliban also enjoyed support from Pakistan, and initially had the tacit approval of the United States. In 1996, they took Kabul.

The movement's international support soon dwindled, however, as their strict version of Islamic law proved harsh. Kabul and other cities outside the Pashtun heartland struggled under the Taliban's medieval rules, but they were not unpopular in Kandahar. The city regained its historical place as a seat of power, and the province enjoyed a stable government for the first time in more than a decade. The Taliban did not provide many services, but they also did not prey upon ordinary people or try to radically reform the social system. Travel was again possible. The Taliban's history in Kandahar as providers of reliable security is a key part of the Taliban insurgency's strength.

Karzai Government (2001-Present)

Many of the figures chased out of Kandahar in 1994 rushed back to regain power after the expulsion of the Taliban. Former governor Gul Aga Sherzai seized control of the governor's palace, and his Barakzai tribesmen became wealthy by providing security, construction, and logistical services to the international forces. President Karzai's younger half-brother, Ahmed Wali Karzai, assumed the chairmanship of the provincial council and emerged as the most powerful politician in Kandahar, especially after Sherzai's final term in office ended in 2005 (Sherzai has since became the governor of Nangarhar province). Mullah Naqib's Alokazai tribe was an important ally for the new government, but their loyalty has eroded since his death in 2007.

The dhol is a traditional percussion instrument popular among Pashtun tribesmen. Working with the local tribes and respecting customs and traditions is essential to effective political development work in Kandahar.

PHOTO BY CPL DAN POP

Chapter 2
Tribes, Ethnicity, Languages, and Religion

ETHNICITY

Pashtuns dominate Kandahar, making up an estimated 98 percernt of the population and marginalizing the tiny minorities of Baluch, Sayyed, Tajik, Hazara, and Qizilbash. The Kuchi herdsmen are a distinct group, though mostly ethnically Pashtun. The Pashtuns are generally Sunni Muslims, as are the Baluch and Tajiks. The Hazara and Qizilbash are Shiites, and the Sayyed are religious families who claim direct ancestry from the Prophet Mohammed and do not fall into either sectarian category. Tensions between Sunnis and Shiites rarely become a factor in this conflict, largely because of the overwhelming numbers of Sunnis. The Pashtuns are believed to be the largest tribal society in the world, with roughly 15 to 25 million people living in Afghanistan and Pakistan. Their code of honor (*pashtunwali*) and related tribal customs are older than Islam, and serve as the cultural bedrock.

Pashtunwali

Society in Helmand is very conservative, strictly religious, and structured around pashtunwali, the code of ethics for the Pashtun tribe. Pashtunwali means "the way of the Pashtuns," and is a pre-Islamic code of conduct

Table 2. Major Pashtun Tribes in Kandahar

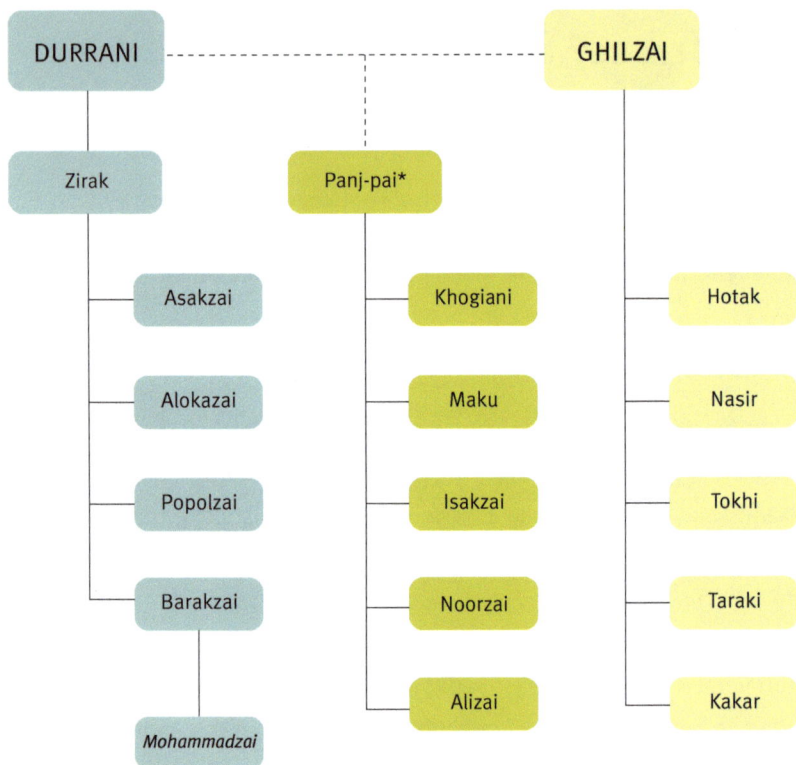

DURRANI		GHILZAI
Zirak	**Panj-pai***	
Asakzai	Khogiani	Hotak
Alokazai	Maku	Nasir
Popolzai	Isakzai	Tokhi
Barakzai	Noorzai	Taraki
Mohammadzai	Alizai	Kakar

Some tribal charts show the Durrani confederacy encompassing the Zirak and Panj-pai groups of tribes, but others categorize the Panj-pai as members of the Ghilzai confederacy. Experience in southern Afghanistan suggests Panj-pai sometimes describe themselves as Ghilzais if they oppose the government or call themselves Durranis if they accept the government.

followed by the Pashtun tribes. All Pashtuns have some knowledge of the code and will try to follow it. Some tribes are stricter about the code than others. The four main parts of Pashtunwali are as follows:

Nang (Honor): All parts of Pashtunwali lead to honor. All Pashtuns are required to uphold the honor of their family and their tribe by following the other parts of the code. An insult to someone's tribe or family can lead to badal (see below). The biggest disputes are over women, land, and money; a Pashtun man must protect these three with his life and honor.

Melmastia (Hospitality): Pashtuns are known for their hospitality and will go to great lengths to treat guests with honor and respect. Most villages and large families will have a dedicated guesthouse. Even if a family has limited resources, a stranger will still be welcomed, fed, and given a place to sleep. This applies to non-Pashtuns as well.

Nanawatay (Sanctuary): If one Pashtun has insulted or committed a crime against another, he is allowed to admit his guilt and ask for forgiveness. He will take gifts to the offended party and ask that the past be forgotten. The insulted party is then obligated to accept the offer. Often the women of a family or tribe will arrange for this to happen because women are seen as natural peacemakers. Nanawatay can also be used to beg for mercy and protection.

Badal (Revenge): Pashtuns are quick to take revenge for an insult or seek justice for a past crime. It does not matter if the insult is decades old. The only way to restore honor to one's family/clan/tribe is to exact revenge on the other's family/clan/tribe.

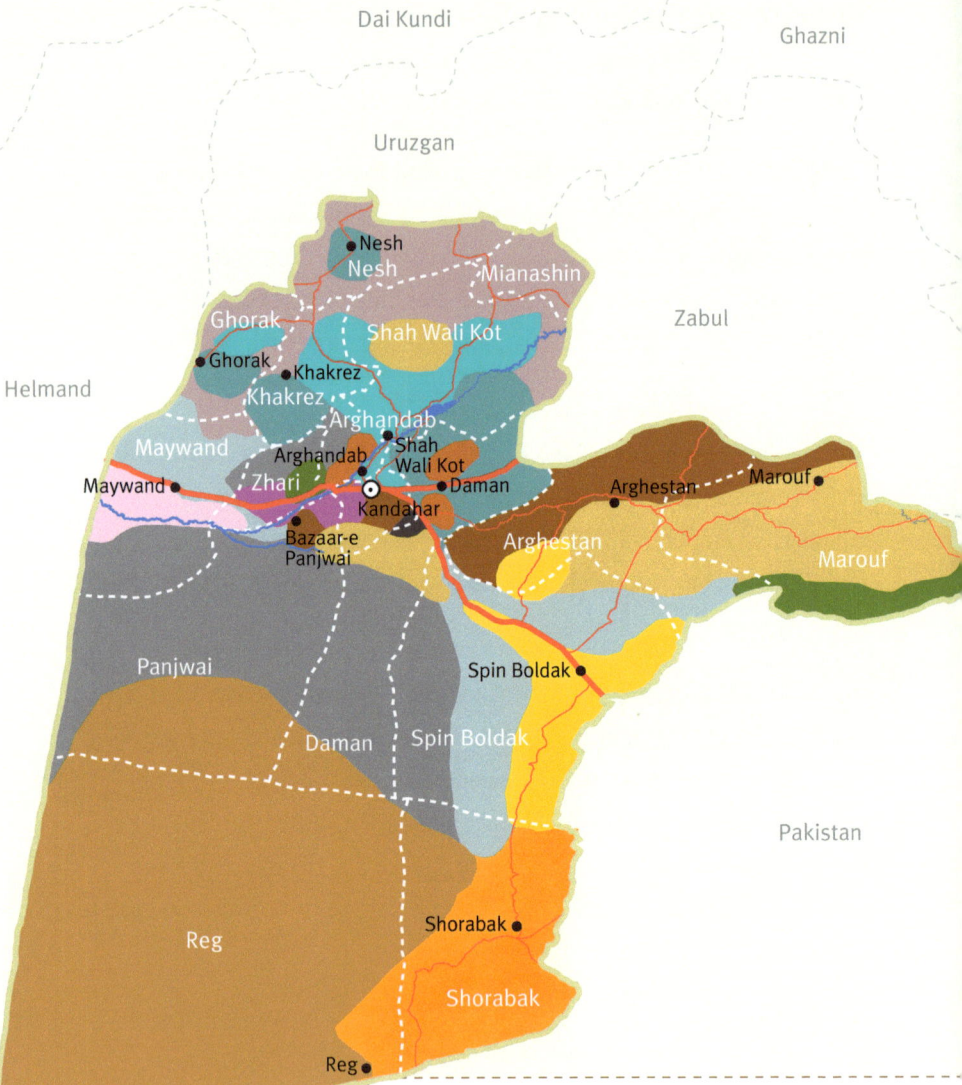

Map 2. Major Tribes of Kandahar

Province/region labels:
Dai Kundi
Ghazni
Uruzgan
Zabul
Helmand
Pakistan

District labels and cities:
Nesh (Nesh)
Mianashin
Ghorak (Ghorak)
Shah Wali Kot
Khakrez (Khakrez)
Arghandab (Arghandab)
Shah Wali Kot
Maywand (Maywand)
Zhari
Daman
Arghestan (Arghestan)
Marouf (Marouf)
Kandahar
Bazaar-e Panjwai
Panjwai
Daman
Spin Boldak (Spin Boldak)
Shorabak (Shorabak)
Reg (Reg)

Legend:

Roads			Isakzai	
District Border			Mixed Ghilzai	
River			Mixed Pashtun	
Provincial Center			Mixed Pashtun, majority Panjpai	
City			Mixed Zirak Durra	
Alizai			None	
Alokazai			Noorzai	
Asakzai			Popolzai	
Barakzai			Tareen	
Barech				
Baluch				

LANGUAGES

Most people in Kandahar speak Pashto, using a local dialect sometimes referred to as the "standard" or "official" version of the language. Translators from other parts of the country often struggle to be understood – or respected – if they have not mastered the Kandahari dialect. Some locals also speak Afghanistan's other official language, Dari, and a few speak Baluchi. Words from Urdu and Arabic have become part of Pashto, but neither language is commonly spoken in the province.

TRIBES

Tribes are the most important political units in southern Afghanistan. They have served as the basis for social organization in the region for centuries, and they remain powerful despite the fact that traditional tribal structures have been undermined by three decades of conflict. The tribes have gained importance in recent years as the government shows weakness and ordinary people look for other ways of organizing themselves. The most revealing question you can ask any Kandahari is, "What tribe are you from?" The answer will give you a clue about loyalties that may cut across any other allegiance to political parties, business deals, or military affiliation. The two basic institutions of the tribal system are the *jirga* and *shura*. A jirga is a tribal gathering to solve a problem or reach a decision, while a shura is a more permanent council of elders who can be responsible for security, justice, and local administration. Shuras can be organized geographically – village shuras are a well-established tradition, while district shuras are a formal part of the Afghan government – and they can also be gathered along tribal lines. Each major tribe in Kandahar has a shura to represent its interests, so you will frequently hear references to the Alokazai shura or the Asakzai shura, for example. Tribal leaders sometimes live in Kandahar or Kabul but depend on their support base in the villages.

Pashtun tribes in Kandahar are broadly divided into three categories, as the chart on page 14 shows.

Categorizing Pashtuns is a bit abstract to most Kandaharis. Nobody would describe himself as "Zirak" or "Durrani;" instead, he would always use his specific tribal name, such as Popolzai. Even smaller divisions within the tribes can be politically important, as the Barakzais in Kandahar have a long-running dispute between two factions of the same tribe, and the Alokazais north of the city are divided over whether they support or oppose the government.

Experts disagree about the role of tribes in the Taliban, but there is a consensus that tribal politics play a role in driving the insurgency in Kandahar. Members of the Zirak Durrani branch of the Pashtun ethnic group, which includes tribes such as the Popolzai, Barakzai, Alokazai, and Asakzai, are generally more supportive of the government than the other tribes. Some tribes in particular – the Isakzai and Noorzai – feel disenfranchised and represent a major source of recruits for the Taliban. This is often described as a result of foreign intervention that has favored some tribes over others in recent years.

The map on page 16 shows which tribes are strongest in broad swaths of the province, but this information should be used with caution. Tribes are scattered across Kandahar in a dense patchwork, dividing districts – and even villages – into distinct zones of control. Rival tribes can hold sway over neighboring clusters of houses in the city.

Major Tribes

Barakzai

The largest tribe by population, the Barakzai, is divided into two major factions. A faction led by former Kandahar governor Gul Agha Sherzai also includes Member of Parliament Khalid Pashtun, Provincial Council Member Haji Mohammed Qassam, and leading businessmen whose wealth comes, in part, from contracts with the OEF/ISAF military forces. The second faction is led by Member of Parliament Noorolhaq Olomi.

Popolzai

The Popolzai are the most politically powerful tribe under the current government. The Popolzai's leader in Kandahar is Ahmed Wali Karzai, chairman of the Provincial Council, who is the younger half-brother of President Hamid Karzai. Other factions of the Popolzai tribe, based in the heavily Taliban-influenced district of Shah Wali Kot, do not recognize Karzai's leadership. Still, the dominance of Ahmed Wali Karzai's Popolzais in Kandahar City is so pervasive that ordinary shopkeepers curry favor with the government by adding the word "Popol" to their business names, such as "Popol's Auto Mechanic" or "Popol's Bakery."

Alokazai

Sometimes called the "gatekeepers of Kandahar," the Alokazai control strategically important terrain in the Arghandab district north of the city and other lands further north. This position, and their reputation as fearsome warriors, has allowed the Alokazai to play kingmaker several times in recent years; their late tribal leader Mullah Naqib gave permission for the Taliban's takeover of Kandahar in 1994 and then served as a key ally to President Karzai after 2001. After the death of Naqib in 2007, his tribe's support for the government has sharply weakened.

Asakzai

Concentrated on both sides of the border between Afghanistan and Pakistan, the Asakzai have a reputation as skilled smugglers. General Abdul Razik, the flamboyant young border police commander, has cemented the Asakzais' dominance over trade routes.

Noorzai

A bitter feud has long existed between the Noorzai and Asakzai in the border areas. Arif Noorzai, one of the tribe's leaders, serves as a Member of Parliament. However, the tribe generally feels shut out from positions of power, and some have taken up arms against the government.

Isakzai

Known for religious conservativism, the Isakzai also feel marginalized by the central government. Their lands in Maywand and Panjwai have been strongholds for the Taliban.

Mohammadzai

This was the tribe of Afghanistan's monarchy, and the Mohammadzai still enjoy an elevated status and a degree of neutrality in local politics.

ROLE OF RELIGION

The vast majority of Kandaharis are deeply devoted to Sunni Islam. Unlike people in Kabul who might occasionally break their religious rules, residents of Kandahar strictly observe the rituals and requirements of their faith. No outsider should ever speak poorly about Islam or accuse an Afghan of being un-Islamic. It is good to compliment someone for being a good Muslim, but the topic of religion should be approached lightly, if at all. Since the Koran is seen by Muslims as an infallible document, delivered to The Prophet directly by God, any debate on particulars of Islamic belief and practice should not be entered into.

Since Afghanistan is an Islamic republic, there is no separation between religion and government. A law must be in line with Islamic principles for it to be accepted. Religious elites have not historically ruled the province, but they have played an important role in legitimizing leaders. Religious figures have intervened during times of crisis, however, and this pattern repeated itself in 1994 when the Taliban seized control and imposed a simple village version of Islamic order during a chaotic civil war. The mullahs lost power when the Taliban were toppled in 2001, and the current government's attempts to bring religious leaders back into the power structure have not been entirely successful. The Director of Religious Affairs (often called Director of Haj and Pilgrimage) is the government's official representative for the mullah community in the province. A total of 89 imams of local mosques are registered with the department, but only 11 of them are based outside of Kandahar City. The official Ulema Shura, a group of religious scholars who support the government, has been heavily targeted in a campaign of intimidation and assassination. Since mullahs are so influential, it is important to reach out to them either directly or through their hierarchy.

Of the eight officially registered madrassas (religious schools) in the province, four have been closed because of security problems. At the same time, there is an underground network of village madrassas that teach more extreme views, and many villagers send their sons for religious education in Pakistan, where some are indoctrinated to fight against infidels.

Kandahar has traditionally produced a wide variety of agricultural products, but farmers now rely more heavily on cannabis and poppy.

PHOTO BY SPECIALIST JOHN COLLINS

Chapter 3
The Economy

Historically famous for its fruit, Kandahar now depends on growing and smuggling illegal drugs for the backbone of its economy. Agriculture and raising livestock remain important industries, but they have been damaged by recent years of drought and war. Kandahar City's position, at crossroads on routes between Iran, Central Asia, and Pakistan, also generates a legitimate trade in transit goods.

Years of drought have been followed by recent hikes in inflation and sharply increased food prices. Kandahar authorities estimated in the summer of 2008 that 6,000 families recently displaced by fighting need help feeding themselves but have received no assistance. Thousands of others depend on help from the World Food Program. Reliable economic indicators do not exist, but anecdotal evidence suggests that rising violence has slowed the economy and left thousands of people unemployed.

INFRASTRUCTURE

Energy

Kandahar City is supplied with electricity from diesel generators and from the Kajaki Dam, a hydroelectricity project under refurbishment by the US Agency for International Development (USAID) in neighboring Helmand province. These sources give the city less than a quarter of the 40 MW of electricity needed to satisfy immediate demand, so residents experience frequent power outages. Many homes in the city have their own diesel generators, but the rising price of fuel has made them expensive to operate. Few rural homes have electricity, although diesel generators are often used to run irrigation pumps. NATO and US forces successfully moved a new turbine to the Kajaki Dam in the summer of 2008, raising hopes that the dam will reach its full output capacity of 51 MW in the coming years.

Telecommunications

Mobile phones have transformed communications in Afghanistan, whose landline system had largely been destroyed and was limited to a few businesses and government offices. Kandahar's residents have a choice between at least four mobile phone companies: Roshan, AWCC, Areeba, and Etisalat. Roshan offers an expensive point-to-point microwave network that connects to the Internet via satellite; AWCC has a more affordable GPRS Internet service that is growing popular in the city. A few downtown Internet cafes cater mostly to young men. Cell towers have become one of the focal points of insurgents, who often interrupt service.

Roads

Paved roads stretch across Kandahar, largely due to internationally supported reconstruction work since 2001. Highway 1 from Zabul to Kandahar and onwards into Helmand province is rough only in places where bombings have left craters. Highway 4 from Kandahar to the Pakistani border is mostly paved, although some sections lack culverts and washed out in recent rainy seasons. New bypass roads are providing alternate routes around the city.

KEY ECONOMIC SECTORS

Opium

Kandahar does not have the vast opium fields of neighboring Helmand province, but the drug lords' lavish homes (known as "poppy palaces," or "narcotecture") attest to the province's importance as a trading hub for narcotics. The UN Office on Drugs and Crime (UNODC) estimated that Kandahar had 14,623 hectares under opium cultivation in 2008, down 12 percent from 2007, but still triple the size of the crop a few years earlier. The recent decrease in cultivation was likely caused by the falling price of raw opium and the rising price of wheat. Growing marijuana has also increased in recent years, as cannabis crops are becoming almost as profitable as poppy. Drug eradication efforts have ignited resentment against the central government, partly because the farmers accuse corrupt officials of using eradication programs to favor growers who have government connections, or to target tribal rivals. These suspicions are fueled by UNODC data, which shows that in Kandahar in 2008, all of the eradicated fields were selected by the governor's office – and 91 percent of the targeted fields were outside the approved eradication zones designated by the Ministry of Counternarcotics.

Agriculture and Livestock

The fruit trees of Kandahar still produce their famous pomegranates, apricots, and peaches. However, many orchards have been destroyed by war, drought, and impoverished people who have cut down trees for firewood. Water levels fell during the years of drought that started in the 1990s, resulting in dry wells and crop failures. This situation improved with good rainfall in the winter of 2006-07 and adequate rain in 2007-08. Besides opium and cannabis, the most common field crops are wheat, grapes, and corn. Farmers also grow cumin, melons, figs, watermelons, and assorted vegetables. Some grapes are eaten fresh, but the bulk of the crop is dried in large mud-walled storage houses and sold as raisins locally or trucked into Pakistan. Kandahar exported more than 2,000 tons

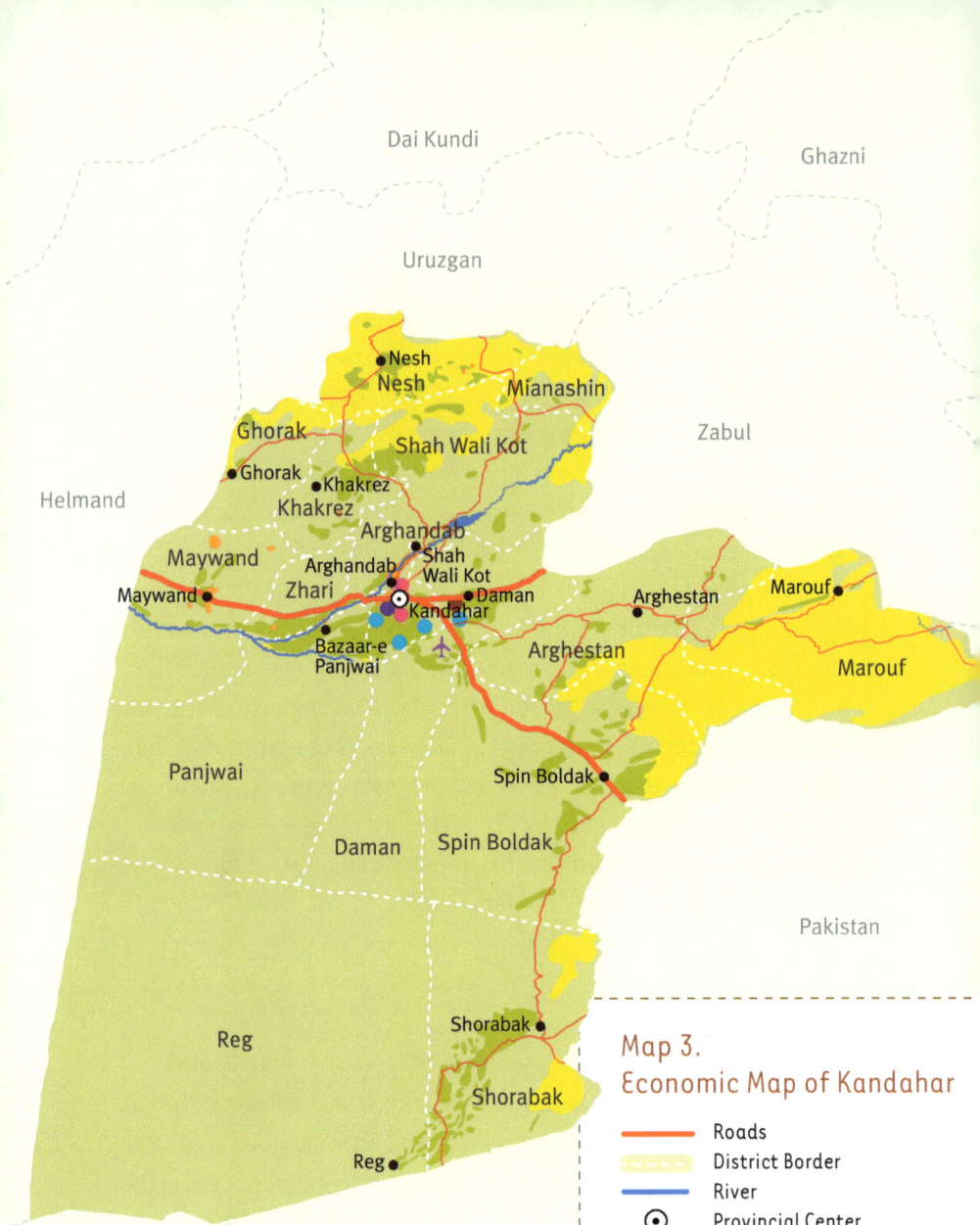

Map 3.
Economic Map of Kandahar

Districts and Places
- Dai Kundi
- Ghazni
- Uruzgan
- Zabul
- Helmand
- Nesh / Nesh
- Mianashin
- Ghorak / Ghorak
- Shah Wali Kot
- Khakrez / Khakrez
- Arghandab / Arghandab
- Shah Wali Kot
- Maywand / Maywand
- Zhari
- Kandahar
- Daman
- Arghestan / Arghestan
- Marouf / Marouf
- Bazaar-e Panjwai
- Panjwai
- Daman
- Spin Boldak / Spin Boldak
- Pakistan
- Reg
- Shorabak / Shorabak
- Reg

Legend
- ▬▬ Roads
- ░░░ District Border
- ▬▬ River
- ⊙ Provincial Center
- ● City
- 🟩 Arable Land (Poppy is leading crop)
- 🟨 Range Land
- 🟧 Fruit Trees
- 🟣 Beverage Bottling Plant
- 🟤 Textile Factory (Not Working)
- 🔵 Stone Quarries
- 🔴 Flour Mills
- ✈ Airfield

of fresh pomegranates in 2008, up from almost 1,500 tons the previous year, in an effort facilitated by USAID. The project made use of a new cold-storage facility donated by the Indian government, but the facility remains empty most of the year because of the fuel costs associated with the cooling equipment. The only fruit cannery in Kandahar was abandoned in the early 1990s, and the building now houses part of Camp Nathan Smith, the military base for Canada's Provincial Reconstruction Team (PRT).

The business of raising livestock is dominated by the Kuchi nomads who shepherd their flocks across vast ranges in Afghanistan, selling their sheep, goats, and camels in the markets of Kandahar. Unfortunately, those herds were also decimated by war and drought and suffer from a lack of veterinary services. In Afghanistan, sheep's wool is spun into yarn to supply the carpet industry. Farmers also often keep a few dairy cattle for their own needs, selling surplus milk to local traders.

Manufacturing

The largest factory in Kandahar is a beverage bottling plant on the west side of the city. It employs up to 110 people and is owned by a businessman named Haji Ahmedy Atiqullah who lives in Dubai. The factory has lost millions of dollars since opening in 2006 and frequently shuts down because of electricity shortages, rising fuel prices, and growing insecurity. The other major factory is a textile mill located on Highway 1 going towards Kabul. Although the machines remain largely undamaged by decades of war, the facility is mothballed, as it lacks the government subsidies and the neces-sary supply of locally grown cotton that helped it employ up to 2,000 people during its heyday in the 1970s. It is unlikely that Afghanistan can ever again compete in the current world cotton market. Smaller industries include stone quarries, steelworks, gravel crushers, ice makers, and a flour mill. The government has designated zones on the outskirts of Kandahar city for business parks. Even after laying roads and raising electricity poles, these areas remain largely empty because basic resources such as electricity and water remain scarce. Investors have not yet been persuaded to start major enterprises in the province. Businessmen have also complained about paying taxes when they receive almost no government services.

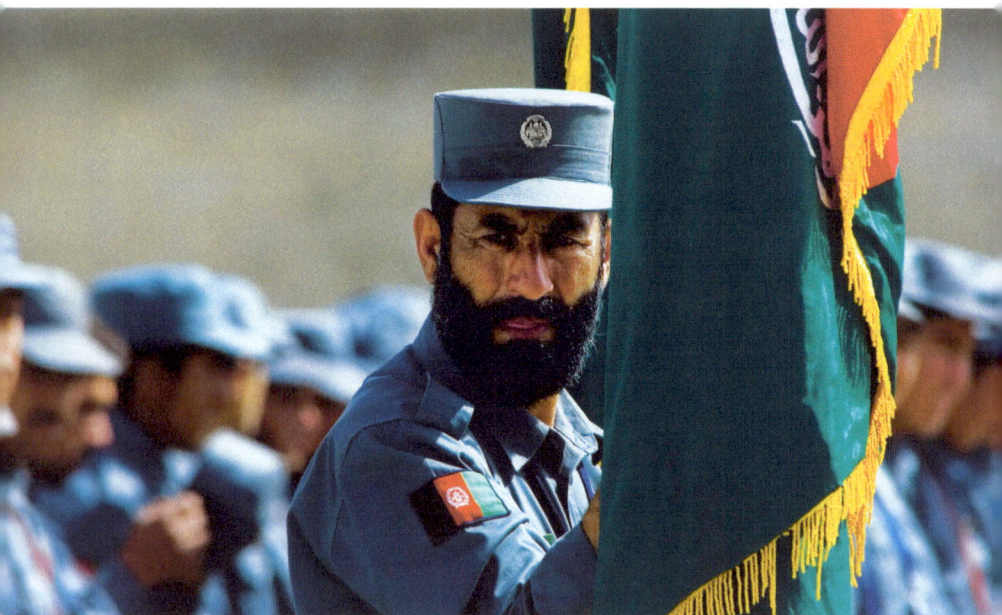

Kandaharis often call the Afghan National Police topakan, or "gun lords," reflecting the negative perception of their effectiveness and corruption.

PHOTO BY CPL DAN POP

Chapter 4
Government and Leadership

Kandahar's governors have been unsuccessful in extending the power and influence of the central government in the province, and locals are widely dissatisfied with their governance. Three parallel systems of government have emerged in the absence of a single effective regime: the Karzai government; the Taliban, who has established policing, courts, and road checkpoints in the rural districts; and tribal leadership, which administers justice and provides security.

HOW THE GOVERNMENT OFFICIALLY WORKS

Central Control

Authority and power in Afghanistan are concentrated in the national government as a means to counter the power of warlords in the provinces. As such, the provincial government is limited to an advisory role for the central government, while decisions on everything from policy to funding priorities are made in Kabul.

Provincial Government

A governor (*wali*) heads the provincial government and reports to the Independent Directorate for Local Governance (IDLG) located in the Executive Office of the president. A deputy and several staffers who oversee the provincial government's management assist him.

Ministries in Kabul execute their policies and programs through departments located at the provincial level. Ministers, with the approval of the president, appoint provincial directors who manage the departments. The director reports to and receives funds from the ministry in Kabul. The governor does not have budgetary authority over any of these departments, but must approve all expenditures before they are processed by the Department of Finance (*Mustafiat*).

The Provincial Council (PC), an elected body at the provincial level, provides a voice for the people in advising on provincial issues. The PC reports directly to the president and has no budget. Its relevance largely depends on the governor's support and on its members' individual resources and initiatives.

The Provincial Development Committee (PDC), including the governor and department heads, is responsible for creating the Provincial Development Plan (PDP) and coordinating with key players on development needs. External players such as the UN, PRT, and interested NGOs also attend meetings.

District and Local Governance

Government at the district level mirrors the provincial government with the *woluswal* (district administrator or sub-governor), police chief, National Directorate of Security officer, clerks, and a small police force. Ministry sub-departments also operate at the district level, but are not present in every district. In 2007, District Development Assemblies (DDA) were formed in order to plan, prioritize and coordinate development activities at the district level. Below the district level, the only formal governance structures are the Community Development Councils (CDCs). These CDCs help MRRD manage the National Solidarity Program.

The municipality of Kandahar City is led by a mayor appointed by the president in consultation with the governor. Municipalities are independent from the provincial government, are free to plan, fund and implement projects, and can tax local businesses.

HOW IT ACTUALLY WORKS – POWER AND INFLUENCE

Governance in Kandahar is a patchwork of competing and parallel systems, carried out among the pro-government officials led by provincial council chairman Ahmed Wali Karzai, the Taliban, and traditional tribal leadership.

The Karzai regime

Ahmed Wali Karzai has become the most powerful man in Kandahar despite his modest formal position as chairman of the Provincial Council. He has used his family's dominance in government and his commercial clout to become the political lynchpin of the southern region. This influence may have resulted in the recent departure of Kandahar's governor, Rahmatullah Raoufi, who served in his post for less than four months.

Ahmed Wali's power has only grown recently as Gul Aga Sherzai, his primary rival and the former governor of Kandahar, was re-appointed governor of Nangarhar in eastern Afghanistan. Ahmed Wali's power was further cemented when Habibullah Jan, an Alizai tribal leader from San Zhari west of Kandahar City, was shot dead in July 2008. Indeed, other members of the Provincial Council have complained that Ahmed Wali dominates the decision-making process. Such dominance stokes resentment among PC representatives of powerful tribes, such as the Alokazai, Barakzai, and Noorzai.

The Taliban

The Taliban control large swaths of Kandahar's countryside. A Taliban "shadow governor" is responsible for the entire province, with subordinates responsible for individual districts, or zones of operation, within important districts. The Taliban's system of government runs parallel to that of the official IRoA sanctioned government: Taliban police their zones of control, arresting bandits, bringing them in front of Taliban courts, and implementing a crude, but reliable form of justice. Villagers often say they appreciate the Taliban's presence because the insurgents protect their opium fields, fight crime, and are not as vulnerable to corruption as the central government. However, people also recognize that the Taliban's strength in the districts has also limited their access to services such as health care and education, and some have moved to Kandahar city to obtain them.

Tribal Tensions and Leadership

With the fall of the Taliban in 2001, a clique of three tribes – the Popolzai, Barakzai, and Alokazai – seized the biggest share of government power. Others, like the Isaqzai and Noorzai, had enjoyed greater prestige during the Taliban regime, and today remain a solid base of recruitment for the insurgency. Despite these allegiances, independent village shuras sometimes administer security and operate their own informal court system without overt cooperation with either the Taliban or provincial government.

POLITICAL PARTIES AND ELECTIONS

Political parties do not play a significant role in the landscape of power in Kandahar. Two power factions have, however, closely resembled non-violent political opposition to the ruling Karzai clan. Habibullah Jan, an Alizai tribal leader from San Zhari west of Kandahar City, forged an alliance with a Tajik presidential candidate Yunus Qanooni. Jan was among the few prominent figures in Kandahar who openly campaigned against Hamid Karzai in Kandahar during the 2004 presidential elections. Jan was later elected to parliament, but unknown gunmen assassinated him in July 2008. Another member of parliament from Kandahar, Noorolhaq Olomi, has joined the United National Front, a coalition of mostly northern parties that has already declared plans to oppose another Karzai presidency.

SECURITY FORCES

Afghan National Army (ANA)

While it is the most respected government institution in Kandahar, the army still suffers from the perception that it is dominated by ethnic Tajik commanders. Some of the best fighters in the army ranks are ethnic Hazaras, whose bitterness against the insurgents stems from the Taliban's ethnic cleansing campaign against them in the 1990s. The strength of the army in Kandahar is officially listed at 6,000 men, but it is widely thought that roughly half that number is serving at any one time. Local residents largely welcomed the establishment of a strong ANA presence in Zhari district in recent years as an alternative to the corrupt ANP. While residents say that the ANA occasionally takes bribes at checkpoints or steals personal items during house searches, the ANA generally avoids the large-scale plundering attributed to the ANP forces.

Afghan National Police (ANP)

Kandahar has had ten provincial police chiefs in the last seven years, as they were successively killed or replaced. The most recent change of command followed the spectacular Taliban raid on Kandahar's main jail in June 2008, in which hundreds of insurgents and other inmates were freed with little resistance from local forces. The ANP officially have 3,500 officers assigned to the province, but police chiefs have often admitted they do not know the real number of those who actually show up for work. A consolidation process has attempted to reduce the number of police forces in the province, which at various times has included the Afghan Uniformed Police (AUP), Afghan Border Police (ABP), Afghan Highway Police (AHP), Afghan National Auxiliary Police (ANAP), Afghan Standby Police (ASP), and associated militia units, such as Matiullah Khan Popolzai's KAU, which patrols the road between Kandahar City and the neighboring Uruzgan province. The police forces have been plagued with serious problems: rampant corruption, drug abuse, involvement in the narcotics trade, and even gun battles between rival security forces. A new training process, known as Focused District Development (FDD), strives to bring discipline to the police forces, but so far with limited results.

National Directorate of Security (NDS)

The inner workings of Afghanistan's intelligence service, the NDS, are not publicly known. Most ordinary Kandaharis are frightened by any mention of the NDS. Residents refer to the NDS using the acronym KhAD, the name of the Ministry for State Security established in 1978 under the communist regime and modeled after the Soviet KGB. A 2004 study found that half of the current NDS staff was also employed by the old KhAD. New leadership was appointed for Kandahar's NDS after the media revealed in Spring 2007 the routine torture of prisoners in custody, and the NDS facility is now also subject to inspection visits by Canadian human rights officials.

Table 3. Wolesi Jirga (Lower House) Members

NAME	TRIBE	NOTES
Noorolhaq Olomi	Barakzai, from a faction opposed to Gul Aga Sherzai	Received military training in the United States in the 1970s; served as a senior communist official in Kandahar from 1987 until 1991. Now a member of the United National Front.
Arif Noorzai	Noorzai	First deputy speaker, related to President Karzai through marriage. Accused of links to the drug trade.
Khalid Pashtoon	Barakzai, from the faction that supports Gul Aga Sherzai	Previously served as an aide to Sherzai.
Haji Amir Lalai	Popolzai	Local commander; gave up some weapons in DDR process. Now supports the United National Front.
Ahmad Shah Khan	Tarakai	Tribal elder from Spin Boldak district.
Obaidullah	Asakzai	Businessman from Spin Boldak district.
Fariba Ahmadi	Kakar	A former teacher and NGO worker.
Shakiba Hashimi	(unknown)	A supporter of Noorolhaq Olomi; she previously worked as a high-school teacher.
Malalai	Isakzai	A former teacher.

Table 4. Provincial Council Members

NAME	TRIBE	NOTES
Ahmed Wali Karzai, chairman	Popolzai	The younger half-brother of President Hamid Karzai.
Mohammed Ehsan, deputy chairman	Noorzai	A close relative of Arif Noorzai.
Haji Aga Lalai	Alokazai	Represents Panjwai district.
Mohammed Yunus Hussaini	N/A	Representative of the Shia minority; businessman who previously lived in Iran.
Haji Nematullah Khan Sherdali	Noorzai	Represents Spin Boldak's large population of Noorzai.
Haji Mohammed Qassam	Barakzai, from Gul Aga Sherzai's faction	Former administrator for the Red Cross at Kandahar's hospital; he is often called "Dr. Qassam."
Haji Sayed Jan Khakrezwal	Popolzai	(none)
Ahmed Shah Khan	Asakzai	Real-estate dealer.
Fazal Mohammed Gharib Shah	Asakzai	Former militia leader from Spin Boldak.
Bismillah Afghanmal	Mohmand	Local newspaper editor.
Janan Gulzai	Barakzai	Former NGO director from Marouf district.
Soria Barna	Tajik	Former NGO worker who previously served with the Department of Social Affairs.
Maryam Durrani	Asakzai	Daughter of a prominent tribal elder.
Zarghuna	Kakar	Former NGO worker and literature graduate.
Sitara	Asakzai	Holds a degree in literature from Kabul University and previously lived in Germany.

Table 5. Meshrano Jirga (Upper House) Members

NAME	TRIBE	NOTES
Mullah Sayed Mohammed	Barakzai	From the district of Daman, he served as a Major General in the communist-era military.
Mohammed Omar Sherzad	Khogiani	Former anti-Soviet commander, worked with the Khalis faction of Hezb-e Islami
Gunga Raam	Hindu	Businessman; represents the Hindu minority

PROMINENT LEADERS

Government Leaders

Governor: As this handbook goes to press in early December 2008, the position of governor remains in limbo. President Karzai has asked Major General Rahmatullah Raoufi to resign. Raoufi had been in the job only four months. Raoufi's removal surprised many and is believed to have occurred because of a feud between Raoufi and Ahmed Wali Karzai, the President's brother. The firing demonstrates Ahmed Wali Karzai's continuing power in the province, regardless of who holds the governor's chair. President Karzai's choice of the new governor can be an important shift in the role and influence of the office and may have some political significance as Afghanistan gears up for presidential elections next year.

Provincial Council Chairman: Ahmed Wali Karzai leads the Karzai family's influence in Kandahar, combining tribal ties with prominence in business and government. His father Haji Abdul Ahad Karzai served as deputy speaker in parliament, but his sons did not inherit the tribal leadership as a blood right. As the younger half-brother of Hamid Karzai, Wali Karzai is sometimes described as jealous of his brother's rise to the presidency. His power grew after his rival Gul Aga Sherzai was finally removed from the governor's office in 2005. The death of his rival Habibullah in January 2008 further cemented the younger Karzai's position. He called a press conference in October 2008 to defend himself against accusations of involvement in the opium trade, a rumor that has circulated persistently for years. He speaks English.

Chief of Police: Sumanwal Matiullah Qati has granted few media interviews since his appointment in June 2008. His predecessor was fired in the wake of a jailbreak at Sarpoza Prison on the western outskirts of Kandahar City. The new police chief claims to have reduced kidnappings and cut the number of robberies 50 percent, although those statistics are disputed by Western security officials. Mr. Qati asserts that he broke with the longstanding practice of police chiefs purchasing their jobs with significant bribes, and earned the posting based on merit. Other sources have indicated that funding for his appointment may have been arranged by Abdul Razik Asakzai (see below), although this cannot be confirmed. He does not speak English fluently.

Head of National Directorate of Security (NDS): Mohammed Qayum Katawazai assumed the job of Kandahar chief for the National Directorate of Security in the summer of 2008 after his predecessor was removed in the aftermath of the Kandahar's jailbreak. He has complained that his department lacks adequate resources, requiring more men and weapons to take timely action on intelligence gathered by local NDS informants. The NDS has also expressed dissatisfaction about supplying intelligence to U.S. and NATO forces without reciprocal sharing from the foreign militaries. He lost his most senior deputy in November 2008 when gunmen – assumed to be Taliban – killed him near his home in Kandahar City.

Members of Parliament: Ahmad Shah Khan is a hereditary leader of the Tarakai tribe. He was a rival of the former leader of the Alizai tribe, Habibullah Jan, who was killed by unknown gunmen in 2008. He serves on the Provincial Council under the leadership of Ahmed Wali Karzai, with whom he is friendly.

Arif Khan Noorzai is a hereditary leader of the Noorzai tribe. His family has been accused of links to the drug trade. His sister married Ahmed Wali Karzai to cement an alliance between the families. Despite his position within his tribe, many Noorzai do not accept his leadership.

Other Key Pro-Government Figures

Qayum Karzai, the older brother of Hamid Karzai, has assumed the role of elder statesman for the ruling family. Born in 1947, he immigrated to the United States and operated a chain of restaurants before returning to Afghanistan and participating in the Loya Jirgas that established the new government. Elected to parliament in 2005, he served on the Narcotics and Moral Crimes Commission but rarely attended parliamentary sessions. In 2008, he gave up his seat in parliament, citing health reasons, and focused on other work, which recently included serving as an emissary for the Afghan government in the early stages of peace talks with the Taliban in Saudi Arabia. He speaks English.

Gul Aga Sherzai has served three terms as governor of Kandahar: first during the brief mujahedin government from 1992 to 1994, and twice after 2001. His final term ended in 2005, and he now serves as governor of Nangarhar. His family has not traditionally held power within his Barakzai tribe, but his father Haji Abdul Latif gained prominence and wealth as a militia commander while fighting against the Soviet occupation in the 1980s. Gul Aga assumed command when his father was killed. His first stint as governor in the 1990s was a notoriously dark period in Kandahar's history, often described as the most chaotic and violent regime in living memory. His second and third terms are remembered more fondly; he was accused of corruption but widely recognized for spreading his wealth. Some of his projects were whimsical – an amusement park, a lavish meeting hall, and an ornate picnic grounds – but also included roads and other public works. His governorship has been criticized for polarizing the tribal politics of Kandahar, patronizing a few favored allies while alienating other tribes.

Ustad Abdul Halim gained minor prominence during the 1980s as a militia commander fighting the Soviets in Marouf district. His power grew as the Russian troops withdrew and the mujahedin fought among themselves; his battles against other anti-Soviet commanders claimed hundreds of lives. He has recently served as a security advisor to the provincial governor. He does not speak English fluently.

Haji Karim Khan inherited a leadership role in his Asakzai tribe from his father Daru Khan. He is a prominent trader, working from his base in Spin Boldak near the Pakistani border.

Abdul Raziq has also gained prominence in the Asakzai tribe recently, using his position as chief of the border police in Spin Boldak district to influence the key commercial routes to Pakistan. He is the youngest man on this list of prominent people and has a reputation for impulsiveness and aggressive behavior. In the summer of 2006 he led an attack against the Taliban in Panjwai district that ignited tribal tensions between the Noorzai and Asakzai, sharply worsening security conditions. He earned praise in June 2008 when his men seized what may be the world's largest intercepted shipment of opium, worth an estimated $450 million.

Anti-Government Figures

Mullah Berader, of the Popolzai tribe, is likely the most influential Taliban leader in southern Afghanistan. US and Afghan forces have twice claimed to have killed him, but he is still alive and continues to serve as the insurgency's chief military strategist.

Mullah Obaidullah, of the Alokazai tribe, a former defense minister under the pre-2001 government, was believed to be procuring new weapons and ammunition for the insurgency. In September 2008, he reportedly organized an ambush that killed three Canadian soldiers west of Kandahar City.

Hafis Majid, of the Noorzai tribe, has at times served as a messenger for Mullah Omar.

ISAF troops on patrol in Kandahar City. Kandaharis respect ISAF for attempting to bring them security and their honesty in comparison to local security forces. Nevertheless, many Kandaharis complain ISAF lacks respect for their culture and traditions.

PHOTO BY LUCAS ROBINSON

Chapter 5
The Big Issues

SECURITY

Security overshadows all other issues in Kandahar. Residents typically express the most satisfaction with security in areas where only one party in the conflict holds ground that is largely uncontested. As of Fall 2008, the largest such zones belong to the Taliban insurgents. Enclaves of government control also exist, such as downtown Kandahar City and the town of Spin Boldak, but these are regularly challenged by insurgents.

Thousands of people have fled their homes to escape the fighting. Expatriates who returned to Kandahar under the new regime are leaving again, and many humanitarian groups have evacuated their foreign staff. Rising instability has resulted in civilian casualties, a lack of highway access, and a renewed role for private militias. Other issues identified in this chapter also contribute to insecurity.

In the last several years, the international community spent millions of dollars on the Disarmament, Demobilization, and Reintegration (DDR) and Disbandment of Illegal Armed Groups (DIAG) programs in an effort to disarm private militias. However, as security has deteriorated, private militias are re-emerging. The Kandak Amniante Uruzgan (KAU) militia, controlled by the Popolzai warlord Matiullah Khan, regularly patrols the highway north of Kandahar to Tirin Kot. In Spin Boldak district, Abdul Raziq's border police units are not formally regarded as a militia but clearly operate as an Asakzai tribal force. Such groups are likely to multiply as authorities search for ways to rapidly increase the strength of their anti-Taliban forces.

Stories of civilian casualties color local opinion of the war. Kandahar's central hospital, Mirwais, receives trauma cases from incidents across the southern region, so the people of Kandahar are regularly exposed to the results of collateral damage. Also, some notorious incidents have involved troops shooting at suspected insurgents as convoys pass through Kandahar City. Planned construction of a bypass road would allow the international forces to avoid driving through the downtown.

The Taliban and bandits have gained influence over the routes outside of Kandahar City, leaving many residents feeling isolated from the rest of the country. This has reduced the ability of aid workers and government officials to deliver services in rural districts. It also threatens the supply of essential goods to military bases such as Kandahar Air Field.

GOVERNMENT LEGITIMACY AND CORRUPTION

The predatory regimes that have dominated Kandahar in recent decades have set a low standard for efficient governance. Many ordinary people would be satisfied with a government that does not inflict too many hardships and maintains a basic level of security.

Insurgents cite a lack of government legitimacy and widespread corruption as reasons for their movement. Even a minor official, such as a police chief for one of the city's ten sub-stations with only a dozen officers serving beneath him, will pay approximately $3,000 in bribe money to purchase his job title because he can exploit his position to make more money illegally.

When it is not corrupt, the bureaucracy is viewed as useless. People who have significant issues to discuss with the government will often go directly to the house of Ahmed Wali Karzai and wait for hours in hopes of getting attention for their problems. The proudly independent people of southern Afghanistan have traditionally lived without a strong central government, and they see no reason to accept the new regime in Kabul if this is all it has to offer.

Many ordinary Kandaharis believe the government's counter-narcotics programs are also corrupt. Villagers do not believe the government genuinely wants to curb the opium industry, but instead wants to damage the farmers and dealers who do not serve the government's own drug cartel. This impression breeds resentment. When police are dispatched to insurgent-controlled districts to cut down poppy fields, their actions are seen as hurting the poor, weak, and tribally disenfranchised. As a result, such actions often result in violence.

The government estimates that half of Kandahar's schools remain open, but the real number may be smaller. School closures are not just a symptom of rising insecurity, but are also a cause. Because Kabul officials write the curriculum within Western standards set by the international community, their schools are offensive to conservative families in Kandahar. Western support of women's programs is a similar problem.

Even the centralized structure of authority, with the governor and district leaders appointed in Kabul, does not fit with the traditional autonomy of local communities. The new government's reputation is further hurt by some recently arrived cultural influences such as pornography in the city markets.

A US soldier trains the Afghan National Army. The ANA is the most respected government institution in Kandahar and residents perceive it as more trustworthy than the corrupt ANP.

PHOTO BY PETTY OFFICER 1ST CLASS DAVID M. VOTROUBEK

Chapter 6
International Community and
Key Reconstruction Activities

The worsening security in Kandahar has made progress difficult for medium- and long-term reconstruction. Many international workers have left as their safety has been threatened. The killing of Canadian diplomat Glyn Berry in early 2006 resulted in strict security precautions for PRT civilian staff, and a Canadian review commission criticized the PRT in January 2008 for channeling more than half of the money from the Canadian International Development Agency (CIDA) through multilateral agencies.

The Canadian military has funded a significant number of quick-impact projects – often basic infrastructure repairs for roads, schools, and irrigation systems – to create short-term employment for local communities and buy goodwill in troubled districts such as Zhari and Panjwai. These short-term projects are sometimes designed to be slow and labor-intensive, emphasizing the benefits of keeping men employed as opposed to focusing on results; the new Mushan road from Bazaar-e Panjwai, for instance, is being paved using simple techniques imported from Africa.

Other projects have depended on the passionate commitment of key personalities, such as the successful pomegranate exporting program established by the US Agency for International Development (USAID).

Programs have also been established to develop capacity in local security and governance structures. However, results have been limited, mainly due to frequent changes in leadership.

PROJECTS AND ACTIVITIES

Electricity

International forces are focusing on improving the supply capacity of the Kajaki Dam in neighboring Helmand province to supply 51 MW to southern Afghanistan's electricity grid. Lack of electricity is a key complaint of local residents when they are asked about the foreign reconstruction effort in their city. Kandahar City currently relies on diesel generators, which produce 9 MW, but they cannot satisfy the city's electricity needs. In Summer 2008, international troops successfully transported a new turbine to the Kajaki Dam, allowing a USAID-funded refurbishment of the hydroelectricity plant to continue. The project may require years of effort, however, as most supplies – including cement – are carried into Kajaki by helicopter to avoid problems on the roads. Nevertheless, even after the Kajaki Dam project is finished, maintaining the electricity lines that stretch along Highway 1 and Highway 611 will pose a significant challenge if current security conditions persist.

Transportation

Since 2001, reconstruction efforts have focused on paving two major highways – Highway 1 from Kabul to Herat, via Kandahar, and Highway 4, from Kandahar to the Spin Boldak border crossing with Pakistan – as well as many smaller roads, including routes from the city into Arghandab, Panjwai, and Dand. Additionally, a new bypass connects Highway 1 and Highway 4. Two other bypasses are planned to the north and south of Kandahar City, a potentially important project that would keep military traffic away from the most densely populated areas. Several other major roads are under construction or in the planning stages. These road improvements have made the highways a target for Taliban attacks.

As the roads become more dangerous, other modes of travel grow more popular. Commercial airlines, including Ariana and Kam Air, operate services from the civilian terminal at Kandahar Air Field, and the flights have become increasingly popular for local Afghan businessmen, government staff, aid workers, and other professionals who must avoid the dangerous highways. In addition, a $110 million railway link from the Pakistani border town of Chaman to Kandahar City was proposed by the Ministry of Public Works, but work has not started.

Irrigation

Irrigation is the largest category of Ministry of Rural Reconstruction and Development (MRRD) spending in the province, and accounts for 95 percent of the laborers hired by the ministry in Kandahar. As of May 2008, the MRRD estimated that the government had spent $3.3 million on completed irrigations projects in Kandahar province, with another $1.7 million spent on current projects. In 2008, the Canadian government announced a budget of $50 million over three years for repairs to the Dahla Dam on the Arghandab River and refurbishment of the associated canal systems. As the second-largest dam in the country, Dahla's irrigation system is believed to support a majority of the province's population.

A vast system of wells, canals, dams, and traditional man-made underground canals known as *karez* is the lifeblood of the province. This ancient infrastructure keeps water flowing to the fields even during years of punishing drought. Many parts of the system have crumbled, silted, or been smashed during recent decades of war, and water tables are falling in Kandahar, making irrigation work one of the major priorities for reconstruction.

Education

The Canadian PRT has invested in upgrades to the infrastructure of Kandahar University, the only post-secondary institution in the province. The university has 1,250 students, including 700 who live in dormitories, despite shortages of water and electricity on campus.

The PRT has announced that it will build, expand, or repair 50 schools in Kandahar, as about half the province's schools are estimated to be closed, while others suffered low enrollment during periods of heightened unrest. In November 2008, attendance dipped sharply among female students in Mirwais Minna, a neighborhood of Kandahar City, after unknown attackers sprayed schoolgirls with acid. Still, 12 girls' schools continue to operate in the province, all of them in Kandahar City. Families in the rural areas often complain that available schooling does not suit their values, and many send their boys to madrassas for a religious education in Pakistan.

Healthcare

Mirwais Hospital is the largest hospital in southern Afghanistan and a major focus of foreign aid in recent years. The International Committee of the Red Cross (ICRC) has 11 expatriate health experts working to establish an emergency department at Mirwais equipped to deal with the high number of war casualties. Additionally, the Canadian PRT has invested in a new $10 million maternity center at Mirwais. Elsewhere, the Afghan Health & Development Services (AHDS) has operated 26 health centers in Kandahar's districts, but its staff has suffered dozens of attacks and several have been killed, forcing the closure of some clinics. The most comprehensive network of clinics in the province is operated by AHDS with funding from the United States, UN agencies, and other donors. With the continued insecurity, many local Afghans travel to Quetta, Pakistan to find better treatment.

THE INTERNATIONAL COMMUNITY IN KANDAHAR

International Organizations and the United Nations

The majority of international civilian staff have evacuated from Kandahar due to rising insecurity. Those who remain are mainly employed by the United Nations, which maintains well-fortified offices and guesthouses in the heart of Kandahar City. The UN's foreign workers are usually forbidden from walking the streets, however, and their visits to rural areas have been increasingly curtailed.

Still, the UN agencies and some non-governmental organizations (NGOs) continue their work by employing local Afghan staff. Private businesses, mostly Afghan entrepreneurs but also a small cadre of foreign contractors, have also become more prominent in the local development field because they are willing to perform risky work for substantial profits. A phenomenon known as "contractor wars" has added to the violence, as implementing partners for development projects try to kill or intimidate their competition. For example, the losing bidder for a road paving project may plant a bomb in a roadway under construction.

Provincial Reconstruction Team (PRT)

The Canadian PRT largely pursued a policy of low-profile development projects during its initial years, investing millions of dollars in support of successful, existing projects such as the National Solidarity Program (NSP) and development implemented by the Afghan government such as the initiatives of the Ministry of Rural Rehabilitation and Development (MRRD). After complaints about a lack of visible progress, Canada announced plans in 2008 to fund three signature projects: repairing the Dahla Dam and associated irrigation system; building, expanding, or repairing 50 schools in the province; and vaccinating 350,000 Kandahari children against polio. Their current relationship with local governments is very strong, working closely with them on all projects.

Since 2005, the Provincial Reconstruction Team has been led by Canada. It consists of about 330 personnel who live and work at Camp Nathan Smith, an old canning factory on the northeast side of Kandahar City. The team is an integrate staff of civilian and military personnel, including diplomats, corrections officials, development workers, military and civilian police, military engineers, civil relations officers, and a company of Canadian infantry assigned to force-protection duties.

The Kandahar PRT, soon to be led by a civilian named in the coming months, is currently headed by Lt. Colonel Dana Woodworth. The civilian leadership includes the Political Director, Development Director, Corrections Director and Civilian Police Contingent Commander. On the military side, the most important players are: the CO, Deputy CO, OC CIMIC, OC Force Protection, S3 / OpsO, and OC SET (Specialist Engineering Team).

NGOs ACTIVE IN KANDAHAR

- ActionAid
- Afghan Disabled Union (ADU)
- Afghan Health & Development Services (AHDS)
- Afghanistan Independent Human Rights Commission (AIHRC)
- Arbeitsgruppe Entwicklung und Fachkräfte (AGEF)
- Area Mine Action Center (AMAC)
- Asian Rural Life Development Foundation (ARLDF)
- Bangladesh Rural Advancement Committee (BRAC)
- Catholic Organization for Relief and Development Aid (Cordaid)
- Catholic Relief Services (CRS)
- Central Asia Development Group (CADG)
- Cooperation Center for Afghanistan (CCA)
- Coordination of Humanitarian Assistance (CHA)
- Handicap International Belgium (HI-Belgium)
- HealthNet International
- Helping Afghan Farmers Organization (HAFO)
- HOPE Worldwide
- Independent Administrative Reform and Civil Services Commission (IARCSC)
- International Federation of Red Cross and Red Crescent Societies (IFRC)
- International Organization for Migration (IOM)

- INTERSOS Humanitarian Organization for the Emergency

- Islamic Relief UK

- Management Sciences for Health (MSH)

- Medica Mondiale (MMA)

- Mercy Corps

- Nye Express

- Oxfam

- Rural Expansion of Afghanistan's Community-Based Health Care Programme (REACH)

- Save the Children UK (SC-UK)

- Southern and Western Afghanistan and Baluchistan Association for Coordination (SWABAC)

- TearFund (TF)

- Terre Des Hommes (TDH)

- Welfare Association for the Development of Afghanistan (WADAN)

Table 6: UN Agency Activities in Kandahar

ACRONYM	FULL NAME	MAIN ACTIVITIES
UNDP-ANBP	UN Development Program – Afghanistan's New Beginning Program	DIAG, Ammunitions – Security
AMAC	Assistance to Mine Affected Communities	Land mine clearance, evaluation and education
UNDP-AIMS	UN Development Program – Afghanistan Information Management Services	Capacity Building working with the PRT
HABITAT	Habitat for Humanity	Rural and urban development programs; National Solidarity Program
UNODC	UN Office on Drugs and Crime	Counter-narcotics, poppy field surveys, drug abuse prevention, and drug control programs
UNHCR	UN High Commissioner for Refugees	Infrastructure, health services and capacity building
WHO	World Health Organization	NIDs (Health)
FAO	Food and Agriculture Organization	Maintaining canal system for agriculture
IOM	International Organization for Migration	Afghan civil assistance; support to provincial government; assistance to Afghan families deported from Iran
UNDP-NABDP	National Area-Based Development Program	Karez and canal cleaning; intake construction for agriculture industry; digging wells; canal rehabilitation; road construction; support to water supply infrastructure
WFP	World Food Program	Cleaning and rehabilitating of roads, canals and karezes; food distribution projects
UNICEF	UN Children's Fund	Provides schools with learning and teaching materials, furniture, teacher training, medication, and sanitation
UNOPS	UN Office for Project Services	Road Construction

American brands and other trappings of the modern world such as mobile phones are visible in Kandahar.

PHOTO BY CPL DAN POP

Chapter 7
Information and Influence

Like the city itself, Kandahar's information environment is a noisy jumble. City residents are deluged with messages from radio, television, billboards and a host of other sources. People wake up to find Taliban night letters posted near a mosque, and soon afterward they're replaced with rebuttal letters from NATO's psychological operations team. A vendor in the market quietly sells Taliban propaganda videos, while another merchant next door offers illicit pornography.

Nobody knows what to believe. After enduring so many covert wars in recent centuries, some Kandaharis are willing to believe the wildest conspiracy theories. Word of mouth remains the preferred source of news, and rumors travel quickly. The best way to elicit genuine opinions from Kandaharis is to sit down with them for long sessions of tea and relaxed conversation. Locals sometimes do not reveal their real feelings about a topic until hours, days, months, or even years have passed.

MEDIA

Kandaharis consume media with deep skepticism, believing – correctly, in many cases – that local journalists collude with the government and broadcast only acceptable stories. On at least one occasion, former Kandahar governor Asadullah Khalid summoned local reporters to his office and instructed them not to disseminate a news item (civilian casualties in Panjwai). The governor's order was followed without exception. Such instructions are usually unnecessary, however, because the majority of Afghan journalists in Kandahar City are pro-government. Their business depends on the survival of a democratic system that encourages media, and, as educated professionals, they face serious personal risks if they travel into Taliban territory. Journalists also know that displeasing a powerful figure can result in grave danger.

Influential politicians control several media outlets while others are state-owned. A more freewheeling discussion of current events in Kandahar has emerged in the anonymity of the Internet, but access is restricted to those who can afford computers and the younger demographic that visits internet cafes.

The media environment is different beyond the city limits, where electricity is limited, illiteracy is common, and people are accustomed to getting information from friends, elders and religious leaders. Despite these limitations, the local media has grown quickly.

Radio

Radio dominates the media landscape in Kandahar because it is cheap and a majority of the population can receive at least a few stations. The BBC's Pashto service is likely the most influential source of news in Kandahar. Other news sources are strongly pro-government: Radio Kandahar is a public broadcaster; Afghan Azada is owned by Qayum Karzai, the President's older brother; and Rana is operated by the Canadian military. Four private Kabul stations re-transmit their signal in Kandahar: Killid, Ariana, Nawa, and Arman.

Music dominates most stations' lineups, but some also host call-in shows, information programs, and news bulletins. Rigorous public discourse and challenging journalism are almost non-existent on radio and television.

Television

Five television stations are available in Kandahar City using just a basic antenna, with two more planned. Ariana, Tolo, and Lemar broadcast the same signal available in Kabul, offering a mix of entertainment and informational programming. The local government station, Kandahar TV, carries some programs from the national broadcaster along with local news and other content.

A more spirited take on daily events is available at Hewad TV, a private channel, which carries news and entertainment – including a sketch comedy show that does political satire. Cable and satellite television are available to those who can afford them.

Newspapers, Magazines, and the Internet

With a literacy rate of 16 to 18 percent in Kandahar, written media is the least popular source of information. The internet may hold greater importance than its readership size would suggest, however, as the wealthy and younger urban classes read a few websites on a regular basis. The internet shapes the views they then pass along using traditional word-of-mouth methods. The most popular news site is www.benawa.com, an online magazine with daily updates and longer features on current affairs. Other popular websites include www.tolafghan.com, www.pajhwok.com, and www.wranga.com.

The largest newsroom in the city belongs to the newspaper Surgar, meaning "Red Mountain," a weekly publication with an estimated circulation of 5,000 to 8,000 copies. Surgar offers the most rigorous journalism among the printed media and conducts regular opinion surveys. The government-owned Tolo Afghan Daily has a smaller readership. Many minor periodicals cover a wide range of subjects, including literature, science, sports, and women's issues. NATO distributes a color-printed newspaper in three languages – English, Dari, and Pashto – but it is not widely read.

INFORMATION SHARING NETWORKS

The informal information networks in Kandahar are not well understood. Taliban fighters in disparate parts of the province have demonstrated an ability to recite identical phrases when asked about political issues. This and other indicators point to the existence of a so-called "mullah network," which appears to efficiently develop messages and spread them across the province.

Westerners are frequently surprised by the speed and reach of news traveling by word-of-mouth; even prisoners in Bagram stay informed about news in Kandahar. The low price and popularity of mobile phones has accelerated this phenomenon. Ordinary people often trust the rumors they hear from their elders or mullahs rather than by paying attention to voices on the radio or television. This has resulted in a Byzantine system of conspiracy theories becoming commonly accepted. Even educated Afghans express concerns that the US and NATO are not genuinely trying to destroy the Taliban and help the average person in Afghanistan. They reason that such a powerful coalition would have already achieved those aims if it pursued them sincerely.

The most widely repeated conspiracy theory is that foreign troops are prolonging the war to entrench themselves in key military bases, which will serve as footholds in the region against adversaries such as China, Russia, and Iran. It is also widely believed that international forces have claimed a stake in the drug trade. Other rumors accuse the foreign troops of immoral behavior.

Kandahar's future is its children. More than half of the province's schools have closed because of insecurity and a perception that Western teaching standards threaten the traditions familiar to conservative families.

PHOTO BY CPL DAN POP

APPENDICES

TIMELINE OF KEY EVENTS IN KANDAHAR SINCE THE TALIBAN'S RESURGENCE

December 2004 – Asadullah Khalid, former governor of Ghazni province, is appointed as governor of Kandahar. He was a loyalist of Abdul Rasul Sayyaf, a controversial figure in Kabul politics.

January-February 2006 – Canada's battle group arrives in Kandahar, bringing the number of Canadian troops in the province to 2,300. The United States hands over lead responsibility for security in the province to the Canadian military.

May 2006 – Taliban fighters show unexpected strength in the Panjwai Valley, southwest of Kandahar City, starting several major battles.

September 2006 – Operation Medusa, the largest offensive by US and NATO forces since 2001, defends Kandahar City by pushing the Taliban out of the northeast corner of the Panjwai valley. An estimated 1,000 to 1,500 insurgents are killed.

Winter 2006/2007 – Following on the tactical success of Medusa, military forces push deeper into the Panjwai valley and establish small outposts.

May-July 2007 – Outposts in Panjwai are abandoned in the face of a growing Taliban threat and infighting among Afghan forces. In the following months, they are re-established and relocated several times.

October 2007 – Mullah Naqib, leader of the Alokazai tribe, dies of heart failure after suffering ill health following a Taliban attack. The absence of this strong pro-government figure hurts security in his district of Arghendab, and reduces his powerful tribe's loyalty to the Kabul government.

February 2008 – A top Canadian commander, Lieutenant General Michel Gauthier, says his troops have been instructed to focus on the core districts around Kandahar City.

February 2008 – Abdul Hakim Jan, a prominent police commander, is killed by a suicide bomber on the outskirts of Kandahar City. More than 100 other people die in the blast, marking it the deadliest insurgent attack to date.

June 2008 – Taliban fighters break hundreds of inmates free from Sarpoza prison in Kandahar City.

August 2008 – Top positions in Kandahar are overhauled following the Sarpoza prison break, with changes to police chief and intelligence chief. Rahmatullah Raoufi appointed new governor.

December 2008 – Rahmatullah Raoufi is removed as governor after an alleged feud with Ahmed Wali Karzai, leaving the post vacant.

COMMON COMPLIMENTS REGARDING INTERNATIONAL FORCES IN SOUTHERN AFGHANISTAN

- International forces try to bring security.

- Kandaharis appreciate the Canadians' restraint in combat, taking care to avoid civilian casualties. (See also common complaints.)

- International forces do not steal from people, unlike local security forces and the central government, and they try to be honest with the Kandaharis.

- Afghans respect international forces for leaving their families to come and help them.

- Afghans compliment the NATO forces' work ethic.

- Afghans appreciate reconstruction projects, such as new roads, that change their lives for the better after decades of war.

COMMON COMPLAINTS REGARDING INTERNATIONAL FORCES IN SOUTHERN AFGHANISTAN

- International forces do not work honestly for security. They are rich and powerful, so they could easily destroy the Taliban.

- Kandaharis say Canadians are not as serious as the US or Russian forces that previously operated in the province because they often fail to pursue attackers as they flee, and do not challenge the Taliban in well-known insurgent strongholds. (See also common compliments.)

- Afghans claim that international forces lack respect for culture and traditions. This includes a lack of respect and understanding regarding women and the way they should be treated by foreign troops.

- Conservative rural people in Kandahar often broadly reject the cultural agenda of the international presence in their country. They feel that girls' schools and similar novelties do not represent progress. They worry that foreigners bring moral corruption.

- Afghans complain that foreign troops enter people's homes without permission, which is a gravely dishonorable act.

- Afghans claim that when international forces are attacked by insurgents, they sometimes retaliate against innocent people, particularly by using airstrikes. Also, they kill too few insurgent leaders, while causing civilian casualties.

- Afghans believe international forces use dishonest informers and interpreters, who have their own agendas, for their intelligence gathering.

- Afghans believe that too much international aid goes to wealthy or corrupt individuals.

- Many people in Kandahar instinctively resent the presence of foreign troops, no matter what their behavior or goals.

DAY IN THE LIFE OF A RURAL KANDAHARI

The life of a rural Kandahari starts very early in the morning with the imam's call to prayer one hour before sunrise. Men get up and wash in accordance with Islamic tradition before going to their village mosque for the first of five prayers of the day. Women pray at home, start a fire, and prepare breakfast. Young boys and girls receive religious instruction at the local mosque after the prayer and before breakfast. In most houses in Kandahar, breakfast is just green tea and bread. This might be supplemented with milk and butter for those who have cattle. Sugar is usually served only to guests.

After breakfast, men go to the field. Families prepare children for school if one is available; schools are more likely in cities and towns than in the countryside. Boys are far more likely to attend schools than girls. If they are not in school, young boys and girls who have not reached physical maturity help to graze the cattle. Children also help with the wheat and opium poppy harvests. The older boys help their fathers in the field.

Migrant laborers are also often hired to harvest poppy, which is very labor intensive. Insurgent activity tends to drop off for about two weeks during this harvest period, usually in April or May. Women do not work outside the home and do not leave the family compound unless it is to visit relatives or attend weddings or festivals. Sometimes on Fridays women meet to sing or recite the Koran. In villages where there is no tension between families, women will not wear the burqa and will speak to men from other families. If there are local tensions, there will often be no interaction between families. Usually everyone returns home for lunch at midday, but sometimes men will stay in the field.

A typical lunch for a Kandahari is rice with cooked vegetables, and is often accompanied by yogurt and slices of onion or other kinds of fresh vegetables from the fields. Meat will be served if it is available. If a family kills a sheep, it will usually share the mutton with its neighbors because the meat will spoil quickly in the hot seasons. Families will usually store pomegranates, almonds, and grapes to supplement their diet during the winter months.

FURTHER READING

- *ISAF PRT Handbook*, 3rd Ed. February 2007. NATO.

- Sarah Chayes, *The Punishment of Virtue*. New York: Penguin, 2006.

- Louis Dupree, *Afghanistan, Princeton: Princeton University Press*, 1979. (Available in paperback and has an excellent understanding of the code of Pahstuns. Understand Pashtunwali and you will be successful.)

- Edward Girardet and Jonathan Walter, *Afghanistan: Essential Field Guides to Humanitarian and conflict zones*, CROSSLINES Publication Ltd., 1998 and 2004, www.crosslinesguides.com.

- Antonio Guistozzi, *Koran, Kalashnikov, and Laptop*. New York: Columbia University Press, 2008.

- Ahmed Rashid, *Taliban: Militant Islam, Oil and Fundamentalism in Central Asia*, 2001.

- Larry Goodson, *Afghanistan's Endless War: State Failure, Regional Politics, and the Rise of the Taliban*, 2001.

- Greg Mortenson, *Three Cups of Tea: One Man's Mission to Promote Peace...One School at a Time*, 2007. (Excellent understanding of how to succeed with the Afghan people and their culture.)

- Barnett Rubin, 1) *The Fragmentation of Afghanistan* and 2) *Afghanistan's Uncertain Transition from Turmoil to Normalcy*, 2001 and 2007.

- Michael Griffin, *Reaping the Whirlwind; The Taliban Movement in Afghanistan*. London: Pluto Press, 2001.

- Steve Coll, *Ghost Wars: The Secret History of the CIA, Afghanistan, and Bin Laden, From the Soviet Invasion to September 10, 2001*. New York Penguin Press, 2004.

- Ben Macintyre, *The Man Who Would Be King, The First American in Afghanistan*, New York: Farrar, Straus and Giroux, 2005.

www.ingramcontent.com/pod-product-compliance
Lightning Source LLC
Chambersburg PA
CBHW040128270326
41927CB00001B/31